In the Beginning God

In the Beginning God

By
John A. Lingenfelter

E-BookTime, LLC
Montgomery, Alabama

In the Beginning God

Copyright © 2006 by John A. Lingenfelter

All rights reserved. No part of this book may be reproduced or transmitted in any form or by any means, electronic or mechanical, including photocopying, recording, or by any information storage and retrieval system, without permission in writing from the copyright owner.

ISBN: 1-59824-287-3

First Edition
Published August 2006
E-BookTime, LLC
6598 Pumpkin Road
Montgomery, AL 36108
www.e-booktime.com

Dedication

This book is dedicated to my dad and mom.

My dad was our protector and provider. He was the decorated soldier, who fought bravely in the Pacific during World War II. He was the father who instilled in us the Judeo Christian based values to live by. He was the dad who took the time to share and to teach my brother Tony and I the various skills that he knew like hunting, fishing, gardening and working with tools.

Mom's legacy is one of faith, hope and love. Her enthusiastic faith, fervent prayer, good example and the scriptures that she so often quoted was the recipe that reassured all of us that we were loved and that we had hope in the future through Jesus Christ.

Contents

Special Acknowledgements 9

Chapter 1 Genesis 11
Chapter 2 The Patriarchs 15
Chapter 3 Moses and the Ten Commandments 18
Chapter 4 The Shepherd Boy's 23rd Psalm 20
Chapter 5 The Nativity 22
Chapter 6 Christ's Ministry 24
Chapter 7 Jesus' First Miracle 25
Chapter 8 Born Again 27
Chapter 9 The Woman at the Well 30
Chapter 10 Bethesda 33
Chapter 11 The Day He Fed Five Thousand 35
Chapter 12 Peter's Walk with Jesus 39
Chapter 13 The Adulteress 41
Chapter 14 Zacchaeus and Jesus Meet 43
Chapter 15 Jairus' Daughter Raised from the Dead 45
Chapter 16 Jesus' Entry into Jerusalem 48
Chapter 17 Jesus Rebukes the Pharisees and Scribes 50
Chapter 18 The Passion and Death of Jesus 53
Chapter 19 The Resurrection and Ascension 66
Chapter 20 The Conclusion 69
Chapter 21 The Prayer of Salvation 71

Special Acknowledgements

I would like to give special thanks to the following people. There were those who wished me well, some gave me good advice, others gave me words of encouragement, provided me opportunity, and there were still others who stood by me during difficult times. No matter in what capacity these individuals may have contributed to my well being, I am better for having known them, I shall never forget them and they are always in my thoughts and prayers.

Ed O'Neill – Ed was my friend's Dennis and Bobby's dad who gave me employment as a teenager in his lumberyard. His kindness and inspiring conversations made my burdens lighter during some difficult times in my younger years.

Benny Cardino - A member of Laborer's Union Local 472 in Newark NJ. He was instrumental in getting me into the Laborer's local which enabled me to earn my way through college.

Johnny Williams - The Business Representative in Carpenter's Local 715 Elizabeth, NJ. John afforded me the opportunity to learn the trade as an apprentice.

James J. Braddock - Jimmy was the Heavyweight Boxing Champion of the world and a work colleague. I had the opportunity to work with Jimmy in 1968. I remember how Jim took the time to talk to me when I was just a young impressionable nineteen-year-old kid. He discussed where I was going to be attending college and wished me the best. Encouragement from a champ like Jim was inspirational and meant more to me than he could ever imagine.

Dick Kleva - My former wrestling coach. Whether an individual was on his varsity, junior varsity or freshmen teams he made each participant feel equally important to the team's efforts. Every member of his staff whether they were assistant coaches, managers

Special Acknowledgements

or trainers were perceived by him as important ingredients that were part of that recipe that made all his team's championship caliber. His enthusiasm and enlightening words filled us with vision. They were instrumental in arming us with the capability to capture the Shore Conference A Division Title and successfully defend it over and over during his eight-year tenure. His pride was contagious as it filled us confidence. His low tolerance for nonperformance instilled in us the notion that we should set our standards high and always do our very best. He taught all his athletes that as long as we were prepared, had vision, healthy minds and moral goals we could hold our heads high and walk with dignity. But ultimately one of the greatest lessons we learned from him was that through hard work and by the grace of God anyone could accomplish that which we once thought was unattainable.

Father John Matejek - My friend and a fellow student from John F. Kennedy College in Wahoo, Nebraska. His example of faith made me conscious of the fact that my faith, that substance of things hoped for and the evidence of things not seen, is truly priceless and that I would never want to lose it.

Beverly Baum-Philback, Roberta Foley, Joan Ciser, Trish Russell and Frank Bertucci - My old friends who constantly reaffirm in my mind the truth contained in the adage that new friends are silver and that old friends are gold.

Donna Kravitz - A special person in my life who has the ability to somehow bring out a better part of me that I never knew existed. The times that we laughed were inspiring and were the greatest times of all.

Tony Lingenfelter - My older brother who in short is always there when I really need him most.

Chapter 1
Genesis
From the Book of Genesis

"In the beginning God",
Are words that most of us know,
They're the first four words of the Bible,
Written over three thousand years ago,

There contained in the book of Genesis,
Genesis means, "origin or beginning" in Greek,
They were written by Moses and were inspired by God,
To provide a way for those who would seek,

But it's hard for people to fathom,
Just how all life began,
To accept God as divine creator,
Is difficult to understand,

The Bible tells us that the Lord God,
Created everything in heaven and on earth,
And that everything was created by him,
Before anything ever gave birth,

He made two great lights in the sky,
He placed them there for a reason,
To give man the signs of the time,
Like planting and harvest season,

To rule the day was the role,
Of the greater light,
While the lesser of the two was there,
Well, just to rule the night,

He created light, dark, heaven, and earth,
Animals that walk, hop, creep and crawl,
It took him the span of only six days,
To finally complete it all,

From the dust of the ground He created man,
And breathed in him the breath of life,
He planted a garden for man to dress and keep,
And to help him, He gave him a wife,

Now the man, his name was Adam,
And his wife, her name was Eve,
After He created and blessed them,
He told them to, "multiply and conceive,"

"Eat from every tree but one," said God,
"And on this you must comply,
From the tree of, knowledge of good and evil,
Do not touch or eat, else the day will come when you'll die,"

There they tended the garden,
And there they would both remain,
For they had not eaten of the forbidden fruit,
So their souls remained both unstained,

There was a serpent in the garden,
Who was as subtle as could be,
He tempted Adam's wife,
And she ate from the forbidden tree,

Then she gave the fruit to her husband,
And thus was the fall of man,
God quickly moved to offer him salvation,
Through a Messianic plan,

In the Beginning God

He placed enmity between the serpent and the woman,
In the form of God's own son,
He'd crush the head of the serpent,
And victory over sin would be won,

He told the serpent that deceived them,
That he was cursed and it was so,
From that day forth he ate the dust from the ground,
And had to crawl everywhere that he'd go,

Then God expelled man from the garden,
So he wouldn't eat from the tree of life,
Or else he'd live forever in sin,
And suffer an eternal strife,

After man was put out of Eden,
Some fourteen hundred years passed by,
And during that time men had taken wives,
And they began to multiply,

But God saw the wickedness of man,
And it grieved him in his heart,
And it repented the Lord that He created man,
So He decided to make a new start,

But there was one man named Noah,
Who had not fell from God's grace,
He told him He'd destroy all living things,
To include most of the human race,

"Noah build an Ark," said God,
"And make it from gopher wood,"
Noah was righteous in the eyes of God,
So he clearly understood,

Then Noah did as God commanded,
And he built a rudderless boat,
It needed no a rudder for steering,
God's hand would guide and keep it afloat,

The Lord said, "I will bring a flood of waters,
So of every living thing take two,
A male and female to keep alive,
Bring into the ark with you,"

Noah and his family went into the ark,
With two animals of every kind,
He knew he was doing God's work,
So he didn't seem to mind,

When his work was now completed,
And everyone was on board,
Noah, his family, and the animals,
Sat and waited on the Lord,

When the Lord saw they were safe inside,
The Lord God shut them in,
It was time for man to pay,
For all his wickedness and sin,

Then the Lord God sent the rain,
And all flesh that once lived died,
It took quite a number of days,
Before the land had finally dried,

Noah had obeyed the Lord,
So God gave him a safe place,
And because of His promise in Eden,
God spared the human race,

Chapter 2
The Patriarchs
From the Book of Genesis

After man had fallen to sin,
And the flood had wiped the earth clean,
The Patriarchs Abraham, Isaac and Jacob,
Took their place on the historic scene,

Now the Lord God told Abraham,
"Get out of your native country,
Go from your father and kindred,
To a land that I'll show thee,"

So Abraham left the city of Ur,
And across the land did trod,
He took all his possessions,
And the faith he had in **one** God,

The worship of many gods had evolved,
After man fell from grace,
Gods of the stars, sun, moon and sky,
Emerged from everyplace,

When Abraham was one hundred years old,
The Lord God spoke again,
He said, "Your wife Sarah will give you a son
Abraham my friend,"

And Abraham believed God,
And God's promise was fulfilled,
Sarah gave him Isaac,
And Abraham was thrilled,

So an old couple who had great faith,
A faith beyond compare,
Made an everlasting covenant with God,
But the story does not end there,

Then the Lord asked Abraham,
To sacrifice his only son,
So he traveled to Mount Moriah,
Where the sacrifice was to be done,

On the way to Mount Moriah,
His son asked Abraham,
"Where is the sacrifice?"
For he did not see a lamb,

Abraham then answered,
"The Lord God He will provide,"
So they traveled to Moriah,
For his God would not be denied,

Abraham had feared the Lord,
And although he was God's friend,
He didn't want to be irreverent,
Or in anyway offend,

So Abraham stretched forth his hand,
To sacrifice his son,
"Because you have feared God," he was told,
"The sacrifice need not be done,"

The Lord God kept his promise,
And he spared Isaac's life,
Then Isaac begot Jacob,
When he took Rebekah for his wife,

In the Beginning God

Gad, Asher, Joseph and Benjamin,
Juda, Levi, Naphtali, and Dan,
Reuben, Simeon, Issachar, Zebulon,
These were Jacob's sons and were all part of God's plan,

They were the twelve tribes of Israel,
And from their ancestral tree,
God would provide the unblemished lamb,
To die and make men free,

Chapter 3
Moses and the Ten Commandments
From the Book of Exodus

Famine plagued the Land of Canaan,
And the people felt hunger's pain,
So Jacob sent his son's to Egypt,
So they could purchase grain,

The Lord God made a promised,
And told them not to fear,
To go and dwell in Egypt,
For He would always be near,

He would make them a great nation,
The Lord God did foretell,
So in the land of Goshen in Egypt,
Jacob's children went to dwell,

Now there rose up a new Pharaoh,
And he knew not the Hebrew way,
He saw God's people multiply,
And he thought there would come a day,

When they would rise up in rebellion,
And be mightier than he,
So he said, "Let us deal with them in a wise way,
And never set them free,"

They had sojourned in the land of Egypt,
For over three hundred years,
And when they fell into bondage,
They anguished in their tears,

In the Beginning God

They cried to the God of Abraham,
To deliver them from their strife,
God looked down and honored His promise,
To give them a blessed life,

God chose a Levite named Moses,
Though of speech he was very slow,
He told him to go and tell Pharaoh,
"Let my people go,"

"I will stretch forth my hand and smite Egypt,
And although Pharaoh will harden his heart,
You will leave with the spoils of the land,
When at long last he'll let you part,"

So God kept His promise,
To the children of Israel,
And they left the land of the Pharaoh,
For their own land to prosper and dwell,

So Moses exited Egypt,
With over three hundred thousand by his side,
And he returned to the wilderness of Sinai,
Where God told him to pitch camp and reside,

Then God gave him Ten Commandments,
For all of His people to obey,
There the foundation of the Judaic law,
And they remain sacred until this day,

Chapter 4
The Shepherd Boy's 23rd Psalm
(paraphrased)
From the Book of Psalms Chapter 23

Around the year 1013 BC,
A little shepherd boy would play his part,
God would later describe him,
"As a man who was after his own heart,"

The young shepherd's name was David,
He wrote many psalms as a young boy,
One of the most famous was his 23rd Psalm,
It still brings the world hope and joy,

David was sitting on the side of the hill,
His job was to guard the families flock,
Sometimes he had scare off the jackals and wolves,
Other times he fed, and tended to the stock,

During time in between, when things seemed more serene,
He'd stop and praise God when things were calm,
And that is why today the world is fortunate to pray,
The young shepherd boy's 23rd psalm,

It goes like this, "The Lord is my shepherd I shall not want,"
When David thought of all he had he'd just rejoice,
"He makes me lie down in green pastures,"
It was then he'd praise God's name with lifted voice,

"He leads me beside the still waters,"
He was always there to guide David's way,
"And through his grace He restores my soul,"
God made David's life a little easier each day,

In the Beginning God

"He leads me in the paths of righteousness,"
Sometimes he needed to know what was right and wrong,
"He does this just for His name's sake,"
David knew that's why they'd laud God's name in song,

"As I walk through the valley of the shadow of death,"
He would conquer David's fears,
"His rod and staff will always comfort me,"
Because His words, they'd always wipe away his tears,

"He prepares a table just for me,"
God would do this in the presents of his foes,
"He anoints my head with his healing oil,
Oh how my cup of blessing overflows,"

"His goodness and mercy shall follow me,
Each and every day of my life,"
And David knew he'd dwell in God's house forever,
Where it was free from any suffering or strife,

Well thank God that David the Shepherd boy,
Took the time to praise the Lord above,
And David knew that if the world would do the same,
It too, could write more psalms about God's love,

Chapter 5
The Nativity
From the Gospels of Matthew, Chapter 2 and Luke, Chapter 2

The prophets they were next,
To be enlightened and foretell,
About a Messiah who would lead his people,
The people of Israel,

Over 2000 years passed by,
From the days of Abraham,
Rome was now the world power,
And they overtook the land,

It happened in 63 BC,
General Pompeii's legions came through,
They occupied the Promised Land,
And dictated what the people were to do,

Then in the year 4BC,
An edict came from Rome,
To tax the world and all return,
Back to their tribal home,

So Bethlehem was restless,
And was as busy as can be,
Everyone was returning home,
Just to answer Rome's tax decree,

The fields and the roads were crowded,
With folks from miles around,
A young couple from the house of David,
Named Joseph and Mary, came into the little town,

In the Beginning God

They came from the village of Nazareth,
Through the hills and back roads of Galilee,
And Mary, she was great with child,
A mother soon to be,

Now Joseph he tried very hard,
To find them both some space,
But no matter how hard he tried,
There was no room any place,

And Mary's time was coming,
To hear it, it seems odd,
That the people were too busy,
That they had no room for God,

So Joseph found a stable
Just a place to keep them warm,
And in that humble setting,
Is where the Messiah Jesus was born,

Chapter 6
Christ's Ministry
From the Gospel's of Matthew Chapter 2 and Luke Chapter 2

So the Messiah was born in Bethlehem,
And yet no one really knew,
Just why he came or what he'd say,
Or what he'd even do,

Now the Zealots thought he'd free them,
Because the Roman's well they were cruel,
They thought he'd raise an army,
And crush the yolk of the Roman rule,

But to love God and your neighbor,
Would be the savior's plea,
The sacrificial offering of animals,
Was no longer meant to be,

With that the Pharisees would get angry,
Because he would preach about God's love,
And he'd claim to be the Son of God,
Sent from his father above,

Chapter 7
Jesus' First Miracle
From the Gospel of John Chapter 2, 1-11

About thirty years had passed by,
And the Messiah Jesus grew,
In body and in spirit,
And he knew what he was sent to do,

It began at a marriage feast in Cana,
In the province of Galilee,
There he performed his first miracle,
And those who were chosen would see,

His brethren, mother and disciples,
Were invited to come and to dine,
It was during the feast that she told him,
That the hosts had run out of wine,

"My time has not yet come," he said,
But deep down in her heart,
Somehow she knew as all mothers do,
That it was time for Jesus to start,

There were six water pots made of stone,
Placed there for purification,
"Do whatever he tells you," she said,
So they obeyed without hesitation,

"Fill the pots with water," he said,
So they filled them to the brim,
"Draw some out for the ruler of the feast,"
That they did, then handed the goblet to him,

He tasted and said to the bridegroom,
"Usually the best wine is served first,
And then the more inferior is put out,
Once men have drank and quenched their thirst,"

"But you have kept the good wine until now,
That's not what hosts usually do,"
But the servants which drew the water,
They were the one's that knew,

The water had been changed into wine,
Though difficult to conceive,
The first of his many miracles took place,
And his followers began to believe,

Chapter 8
Born Again
From the Gospel of John Chapter 3, 1-21

It was during his inaugural year,
He traveled south from the Province of Galilee,
And he headed toward Jerusalem,
Where he met up with a Pharisee,

His name was Nicodemus,
He was a leader of the Jews,
He was searching for Jesus of Nazareth that night,
Because he felt somewhat confused,

It was evening about the ninth hour,
And the sun was well at rest,
Nicodemus had ended a busy day,
Of just trying to do his best,

He finally found him late that night,
He too, had a busy day,
He had taught and healed many people,
And the crowds had now gone their way,

He approached him while he was sleeping,
He would greet him in a respectful way,
Because he heard him teach and saw the miracles,
That he had done on that very same day,

Jesus was at rest now,
When he humbly made his approach,
He didn't want to disturb him,
Or in anyway encroach,

Then master opened up his eyes,
Smiled, and then did say,
"You look somewhat confused my friend?
May I help you find your way?"

"Rabbi, we know you are a teacher from God,
And we know that He is with you,
Else no man can do these miracles,
That you so often do,"

"Except a man is born again,
He can't see God's kingdom," he told the Pharisee,
Born again? He thought, born again?
Just how can these things be?

"Can a man reenter his mother's womb?
And once again be born?"
At this he was even more confused,
And his heart was more forlorn,

"Except a man is born of water and spirit,
God's kingdom, he'll never see,"
The difference between being born of flesh and spirit,
He explained to the Pharisee,

"When the wind blows you hear its sound,
And where it came from you don't know,
For there's no man who can see the wind,
Nor can he see where it may go,"

"When I tell you of these earthly things,
And yet you don't believe,
How can I tell you of heavenly things,
Which are much harder to perceive?"

In the Beginning God

"Moses lifted up the serpent in the desert,
So must it be with the Son of Man,
He will open the door to salvation,
For this is all part of God's plan,"

"For God sent not his son to condemn the world,
But that through him the world might be saved,
And if you believe he suffered and died for your sins,
Then your road to his kingdom is paved,"

Chapter 9
The Woman at the Well
From the Gospel of John 4, 6-40

For the time, his work in Judea was done,
So he traveled north with his men,
He was on his way to Galilee,
Where he would try to preach in his hometown again,

He needed to pass through Samaria,
And it wasn't a friendly place,
The Jews thought the Samaritan's were half-breeds,
And that they weren't really in God's grace,

At the edge of the village of Sychar,
He sat on Jacob's well to rest,
He had sent his men to buy food,
It was there he made an unusual request,

A Samaritan woman scorned for her lifestyle,
Came to the well each day,
She preferred to come when no one was there,
Draw water and then go her way,

"Give me a drink," he asked her,
She said, "You know we have nothing to do with you,"
He had ignored social customs, crossed racial barriers,
And she didn't know what to do,

"Sir you know that Jews have no dealings with Samaritans,
To even speak would cause us disgrace,
And yet you ask a drink of me,
Sir you put me in an awkward place,"

In the Beginning God

"If you only knew God's gift", said he,
"And what He would like to do,
You would ask him to give you a drink,
And He would bestow Living Water to you,"

"Sir you have nothing to draw with,
And the well is deep," said she,
"From where does this living water flow?
This is really all beyond me,"

"If you drink from this well, you will thirst again,
But not from the water I give,
For within you will spring up a well so great,
That an eternal life you shall live,"

"Sir give me this water, so I'll never thirst,
Nor will I ever need to come to this place,"
He said, "Get your husband," as if to imply,
So you both can share, "Go, quickly, make haste,"

"I have no husband," the woman replied,
"Thou hast answered well," said he,
"The fact of the matter you have had five,
And the man you are with, is not your husband I see,"

She felt uneasy about all that he knew,
Yet she felt compelled to say,
"Sir, I see you're a prophet,
So I'll ask just one question of you today,"

So she asked him about on old issue,
Debated by Samaritan and Jew,
If he was truly a prophet she thought,
He will know just what to do,

"Where should God be worshipped?
In our shrine at Mount Gerizim as we Samaritans do,
Or is it in the temple at Jerusalem,
As is practiced by the Jew?"

He looked on her with compassion,
For she really wanted to know,
Then he said, "Neither in Jerusalem nor in this place,
Is where you need to go,"

"It isn't where you worship,
But it only matters how,
You must worship the Lord in Spirit and Truth,
And that time has come right now,"

"I know Messiah is coming,
He'll explain and then we will see,"
Then he answered her and softly replied,
"I who speak to you am He,"

It was the first time in public he'd told anyone,
That he was the Christ, anointed by God from above,
And he told her, a social outcast,
She was so moved by God's love,

Then she left the well all excited,
And told everyone she could tell,
About the man who told her about her life,
And that she met him at Jacob's well,

The people asked him to stay on,
So he stayed for two more days,
He preach the Gospel of good news to them,
And then continued north on his way,

In the Beginning God

Chapter 10
Bethesda
From the Gospel of John Chapter 5, 2-9

It was the second year of his ministry,
During the feast of the Jews,
Jesus came back to Jerusalem,
And there he would make more news,

A paralyzed man inflicted with disease,
Had suffered for thirty eight years,
By the sheep gate, near the pool at Bethesda,
Is where he anguished and shed his tears,

The pool was named Bethesda,
It meant, "Having five porches," in the Hebrew tongue,
Folks with all kinds of illnesses lay by the pool,
Some were old and some were young,

At a certain season an angel came down,
Troubled the waters and then went his way,
And the first one who stepped into the water,
Was made whole of their disease that day,

When Jesus came by he saw the man,
He knew he'd been a long time in that case,
Then he asked, "Wilt thou be made whole?
And take your bed and leave this place?"

He replied, "Sir I have no man to help me,
So each year I lie stricken in this bed,
For each time I try to get into the pool,
Someone steps in front of me and goes ahead,"

Then Jesus said, "Rise take up thy bed and walk,"
Then he slipped into the crowd and went his way,
And the man who suffered for thirty-eight years,
Was cured instantly that day,

As he took up his bed he was reminded,
That it was the Sabbath day,
The Leaders inquired, "Who told you that it was lawful,
To take your bed and carry it away?"

"It was he that made me whole,"
That said, "Take up thy bed and walk,"
But he couldn't even give them Jesus' name,
For they never had time to talk,

The Nazarene had humbly gone away,
To avoid the crowds in that place,
It was later Jesus found him in the temple,
And there they met face to face,

He told him, "Because thou art made whole,
And from suffering you are free,
Go your way and sin no more,
Lest something worse come unto thee,"

Then he told the Leaders who inquired,
That he had done his father's will,
And it was lawful to do good deeds on the Sabbath,
And to cure all those who were ill,

"You believe the scriptures lead to eternal life,
And yet you cannot see,
They were written by Moses to tell of God's plan,
And it was Moses who wrote of me,"

Chapter 11
The Day He Fed Five Thousand
From the Gospels of Mark 6, Luke 9 and John 6
(The fisherman is a fictitious character but the feeding of Five Thousand is contained in the Gospels.)

During the third year of his ministry,
There was fisherman, who was feeling blue,
Early morning he walked through Bethsaida, to his boat,
Just like he would always do,

He looked to the sky and wondered why,
There was something missing in his life,
Oh he made a living with his little boat,
Fed his kids and loved his wife,

The ancient fight between day and night,
That was drawing to an end,
This time night was found to be in retreat,
So that meant his work would soon start again,

So he hoisted the sail to get underway,
And just then, he heard the crowd,
They were following a man from Galilee,
And their cries for help were loud,

Some came, because they saw the miracles,
Others asked him to ease their pain,
He climbed up the side of the mountain,
So he could see them and meet their needs once again,

Well the fisherman dropped the sail and anchored,
Just to see what he could see,
He thought what made this man so popular?
This carpenter from Galilee,

He followed him up the side of the hills,
And made his way through the crowd,
They were like sheep without a shepherd,
And their cries grew increasingly loud,

So he found a place and then he sat down,
Just to hear what he had to say,
But he never thought his words and his deeds,
Would change his life so much that day,

The people came from miles around
To be healed and hear him teach,
He taught with such authority,
Like none other he'd ever heard preach,

Passover feast took place that week,
So he was in the mood to hear him talk,
Oh he preached about God's kingdom,
And taught them all how to walk life's walk,

Later an old man and a young boy sat on each side of him,
And they stayed though out the day,
When the old man wasn't looking,
He saw him bow his head with a teary eye and pray,

Together they sat, listened and then watched,
As he healed all the sick, the blind and lame,
Oh he healed each and every one of them,
He treated everyone the same,

In the Beginning God

The time passed by so swiftly,
And when the day was far spent,
He asked his men to feed the crowd,
But they didn't know quite what he meant,

"There's a lad here with two small fishes,"
His disciple Andrew said,
"He also has five barley loaves, but what are these among so many?
Should we ask him for his fish and bread?"

The little boy heard and came forward in faith,
To share all that he had, he nodded at the boy,
And with a smile and a wink,
Accepted the gift from the tiny lad,

Then he smiled again and he looked to the sky,
Then he blessed the fish and bread,
And because of a little boy's faith and his love,
All five thousand there were fed,

After they ate, he wanted to dismiss the crowd,
Because he knew they'd crown him king,
But first, he told his men pick up the fragments,
And be sure not to waste anything,

In all, twelve baskets were gathered up,
Then he sent the people away,
He himself departed to the mountaintop,
It was there that he went to pray,

It was the day he fed five thousand,
And the fisherman learned a great lesson that day,
That he too, should have that childlike faith,
As he walked along life's way.

John A. Lingenfelter

He healed so many people, after everyone left,
The fisherman sat alone on the hillside and cried,
It was the day that he fed five thousand,
And not one person was denied,

Chapter 12
Peter's Walk with Jesus
From the Gospel of Matthew Chapter 14

His work for the day was now complete,
And his men gathered up the food,
So that none of it would be wasted,
After he had fed the multitude,

Twelve baskets of fragments were gathered up,
From the feast they had that day,
Then he told his men to get into the ship,
While he sent the crowds on their way,

He climbed up the side of the mountain,
To talk to his father in prayer,
He told his men to cross over the lake,
And he would later join them there,

When evening came, he was alone in prayer,
While his men were still at sea,
Both the wind and waves were rough now,
So their ship was tossed violently,

In the fourth watch of that evening,
He came, walking on top of the sea,
They cried out in fear, "It's a spirit!"
And he said "Fear not, it's me,"

Peter looked with his eyes wide opened,
And said, "Lord bid me to come if that's you,"
And Jesus said, "Come," and with that reply,
Peter walked on the water too,

When his eyes were focused only on Jesus,
He too walked on that turbulent sea,
But when he saw the waves were high, he cried out,
"Lord I'm sinking come and save me!"

Jesus quickly stretched forth his hand,
He caught him and pulled Peter out,
And asked, "At what part of your walk with me,
Did you begin to doubt?"

Together they walked to the ship,
As he held tight to Jesus' hand,
Then they climbed up the side and boarded,
And they were on their way to dry land,

His men in the vessel rejoiced,
And proclaimed him to be God's own son,
Then they landed on the shore of Gennesaret,
Where there was much more work to be done,

Chapter 13
The Adulteress
From the Gospel of John Chapter 8

He had returned to the Mount of Olives,
And came early to the temple to teach,
The people came unto to him,
To listen to him preach,

A woman was brought before him,
By the Pharisees and the Scribes,
She was accused of breaking the Mosaic Law,
That was sacred to Israel's tribes,

"Master this woman's an adulteress,
She was caught in the very act,
The law says that she must be stoned,
And you know that this is a fact,"

"Well now you've heard the story,
And we'd like to know what you think,"
But he stooped down and ignored them,
And he didn't even blink,

Then with his index finger,
He began to write upon the ground,
And the people stood there looking,
And you didn't hear a sound,

For awhile there was just silence,
And then they pressed him for a reply,
"She was taken in the act of adultery,
And this she doesn't deny,"

He answered, "He that is without sin,
Let him be the first to cast a stone,"
Even though she was the center of attraction,
She trembled in fear and felt so all alone,

Then he stooped again to the ground,
And once more began to write,
She knew her life was in jeopardy,
And she never had such a fright,

Although surrounded by accusers,
There was tad of hope that she felt,
As the Nazarene though he hardly spoke,
Continued to write as he knelt,

Her accusers left her one by one,
Until they both stood there alone,
There was none left to accuse her,
Or to cast at her the first stone,

Their conscience had convicted them,
From the eldest to the last,
It seemed to her an eternity,
But it all happened very fast,

"Where are your accusers?
Hath no man condemned thee?"
"No man Lord," was her reply,
"And neither do I," said he,

As she sobbed from fright and embarrassment,
She got up from the temple floor,
Then he looked at her and forgave her,
And said, "Go, and sin no more,"

Chapter 14
Zacchaeus and Jesus Meet
From the Gospel of Luke Chapter 19

Later Jesus was passing through,
The town known as Jericho,
And the people crowded into the streets,
To see which way he would go,

By now they knew him in every province,
And in the villages throughout the countryside,
His fame had spread throughout the land,
And he was now known nationwide,

Those who heard him preach before,
Wondered if he would speak today,
Others asked would he do some miracles,
Or just continue on his way?

A man named Zacchaeus sought to see him,
And Zacchaeus was very small,
And the crowds they were in front of him,
So he couldn't see Jesus at all,

So he ran ahead before him,
And climbed up a sycamore tree,
He knew Jesus would soon pass by,
And he'd get his chance to see,

As Jesus passed he looked up,
And he saw him in the tree,
He said, "Zacchaeus, make haste, come down,
Today I need to abide with thee,"

Now Zacchaeus was a sinner and tax collector,
And was not held in high esteem,
Yet Jesus chose to reside with him,
As odd as it all may seem,

So he made haste and climbed down,
And he received him joyfully,
Then he asked, "Lord please come to my home,
And have dinner with my family,"

Jesus accepted his offer,
And the people began to complain,
They asked, "Why does he dine with sinners?"
And they looked at them both with distain,

Zacchaeus was quickly converted,
And promised to repay fourscore,
Any money he had taken dishonestly,
From anyone else before,

He also made a promise,
To give half of his goods to the poor,
He was no longer the greedy little man,
That he had been once before,

Then Jesus said, "Truly salvation,
Has come to this house this day,"
And he and his men went into his home,
And they all enjoyed their stay,

Chapter 15
Jairus' Daughter Raised from the Dead
From the Gospels of Matthew, Chapter 9 Mark, Chapter 5

Whether people loved him or were offended,
When he passed by they'd gather to see,
The carpenter, the miracle man,
From the province of Galilee,

At that time Jairus a synagogue ruler,
Came to Jesus and said,
"My twelve year old daughter was very ill,
And now she lies at home and is dead,"

"If you come lay your hands upon her,
I know that she'll live again,"
So Jesus arose and followed him,
And so did all of his men,

And a woman with a blood disease,
That she had for twelve long years,
Came to touch his garment,
As she anguished in her tears,

She tried many physicians,
And spent everything she had,
Her condition only grew worse,
And she was feeling very bad,

"If I could only touch his garment,"
She believed deep within her soul,
That her blood disease would go away,
And she would be made whole,

John A. Lingenfelter

She made her way through the crowed street,
And followed him close behind,
Touching the hem of his garment,
Was the only thing on her mind,

He turned from the crowd when she touched him,
And said, "Daughter be of good cheer,"
He also looked at Jairus and smiled,
Because he didn't want him to fear,

She was cured that very hour when he said,
"Thy faith hath made thee whole"
And she never felt so good before,
Both in body and in soul,

When Jesus came into Jairus' house,
It was true his daughter had died,
The minstrels made their noises,
And the family sat and cried,

"The maid she only sleeps," said he,
And with that they laughed him to scorn,
Everyone looked at him in shock,
As the family was grieved and torn,

Then he put everyone out of the house,
Except her mom and her dad,
He said, "Peter, James, John you stay on!"
They nodded and all were so sad,

Then he took the maiden by her hand,
And he told her, "Maid arise,"
With that her spirit had returned,
And she opened up her eyes,

In the Beginning God

He conquered the sting of death that day,
And spared the family from grief,
And he did by taking authority,
When he removed all the unbelief,

Chapter 16
Jesus' Entry into Jerusalem
From the Gospel of Matthew 21

Passover feast was coming,
And his time was coming near,
He made his way back to Jerusalem,
And his men began to fear,

He spoke how the son of man,
Would be given to the Pharisees,
To suffer and be put to death,
To fulfill the prophesies,

And Peter said, "Not so Lord,"
But he rebuked him when he said,
"Peter you savor the things of the world,
Savor the things of God instead,"

When they drew nigh unto the city, he said,
"There is a colt there that is tied,
Loose him and bring him to me",
And he told them they'd not be denied,

"If anyone should ask you,
Tell them the Lord hath need of him,"
And his men did as instructed,
And he entered Jerusalem,

When he rode into city,
The prophecy was fulfilled,
Israel's king came meekly sitting on an ass,
And the people were ever so thrilled,

In the Beginning God

The multitudes paid him homage,
As they hailed him prophet and king,
"Hosanna to the son of David,"
They all began to sing,

"Blessed is he that cometh,
In the name of the Lord,
Hosanna in the highest!"
They shouted in one accord,

They cut branches from the palm trees,
And placed them and their garments in his way,
"Hosanna in the highest!"
Were the words of praise that day,

Then he went into temple and proclaimed,
His father's house a house of prayer,
He cast out those that made profits,
From money that was exchanged there,

The blind and lame came unto him,
And many fell down on their knees,
He healed them as they cried, "Hosanna,"
And the Leaders were very displeased,

The leaders saw everyone praise him and asked,
"Do you hear what the people say?"
"Even babies will praise the Son of Man,"
Would be his answer to them that day,

But what lie ahead the remaining week,
For the son of man,
Would open the door to salvation,
And would complete God's glorious plan,

Chapter 17
Jesus Rebukes the Pharisees and Scribes
From the Gospel of Matthew Chapters 22 and 23

Jesus saw that as time had passed,
The Leaders had perverted the Mosaic Law,
So frequently he pointed out,
The inconsistencies that he saw,

He came to Jerusalem's temple,
And the people flocked like birds,
The Pharisees sent some men that day,
To try and trap him in his words,

They asked, "Should we pay the Romans their taxes?
We know you're honest and true,
Now we'd like to have an answer,
As to what **you** think we should do,"

Then he asked them for a coin,
And they handed him the same,
"Whose image is on the coin?" he asked,
"And what is the figures name?"

They all replied, "Caesar's"
And they responded in one accord,
He answered, "Give to Caesar what is his,
And to the Lord what belongs to the Lord,"

He told the people, "The Pharisees,
Sit in Moses seat, so do the things they say,
But be careful not to follow their example,
And walk in their sinful way,"

In the Beginning God

Then he accused them of placing great burdens,
Upon the backs of men,
He told the Leaders they were hypocrites,
Over and over again,

He said, "You don't even lift your finger,
To try and practice what you say,
But you love the special treatment,
That you receive in public each day,"

"The best seats at the banquets,
At temple your private pew,"
He disagreed with their titles Rabbi and Father,
And with their personal points of view,

"You evict widows from their homes,
Then they have no where to dwell,
You go to great length to make converts,
Then make them twice as fit for hell,"

"The more service you give to others,
The greater you might be,
But your pride makes you blind leaders,
And that's the reality,"

"You strain at a gnat and swallow a camel,
Yet you don't think it's a flaw,
When you look at only the letter,
And ignore the very heart of the law,"

"Your fathers killed the prophets,
And you have the nerve to say,
If a prophet came to you,
You wouldn't treat them the same way,"

He called them, "A brood of vipers,"
That didn't do their job well,
Then he asked them,
"How do you expect to escape the judgment of hell?"

Then he walked out of the temple,
When he reproved them all that day,
And warned them with this statement,
As he turned and walked away,

"You shall not see me henceforth!"
And his words cut like a sword,
"Until you say, blessed is he,
That cometh in the name of the Lord!"

So Jesus left the temple,
After he rebuked their evil ways,
To celebrate the Passover feast,
That was to begin in two more days,

Chapter 18
The Passion and Death of Jesus
From the Gospels of Matthew, Chapters 26,27 Luke, Chapters 22, 23 and John Chapters 11, 12, 18, 19

Jesus was called to Bethany,
Where he raised Lazarus from the dead,
Many people believed on him,
And that the Leaders did dread,

The multitudes revered him,
And called him Israel's king,
The leaders said it would infuriate Rome,
And that this was a dangerous thing,

So they called the council together,
To discuss the issue at hand,
They thought it better for one man to die,
Than for Rome to destroy their land,

Meanwhile at Simon the leper's home,
He sat with his men to eat,
A woman with a costly jar of ointment,
Came and poured it on his head and feet,

When his men saw what she had done,
They all became quite sore,
"The money from the sale of the ointment,
Could have been given to the poor,"

"The poor you will have with you always,
But you'll not always have me,
She has prepared me for my burial," he replied,
"And this will be told in her memory,"

From that time on one of his men Judas,
Plotted to turn him in,
Jesus was getting closer,
To conquering all of sin,

The chief priests, scribes and leaders,
Gathered at the palace of the high priest,
They consulted about how to arrest him,
But not on the Passover feast,

Meanwhile, Peter and James were told,
"Prepare a place for us to meet,"
So in an upper room they made arrangements,
For the Passover feast to eat,

When the hour was come they all sat down,
To the feast of unleavened bread,
"One of you will betray me,"
Those were the words that he said,

With that they all inquired,
Just who the trader might be,
"He who dips his hand with me in the dish,
He's the one who'll betray me,"

With that Judas dipped in the dish,
And asked, "Master is it I?"
Jesus answered, "Thou hast said, now go,"
And Judas left without reply,

Then Jesus took the bread,
Blessed it, and broke the same,
"This is my body to be given,
For man's sins it will bear the blame,"

In the Beginning God

Likewise he took the cup of wine,
Gave thanks and divided it among his men,
And said, "I will not drink of the fruit of the vine,
Until I drink with my Father again,"

"This cup is a symbol of the New Testament,
An agreement between God and all men,"
And the testament still stands today,
Until he will come again,

Then he rose from the table,
After they all did eat,
And he began one by one,
To wash his disciples feet,

When he came to Peter, Peter asked,
"Why would you wash me?"
"Right now Peter, you don't understand,
But later on you'll see,"

"I must wash you clean," said Jesus,
"And I know you don't see,
But if you do not let me wash you,
Then you'll have no part of me"

His men really didn't comprehend,
But later on they would know,
He had to cleanse man from his sins,
So his sacrificial blood had to flow,

Peter said, "Lord I would die for you,"
And he told him, "That's not so,
Tonight you'll deny three times that you know me,
Before the cock twice will crow,"

Then he crossed the Kidron Valley,
And his disciples came along too,
And they made their way to Gethsemane,
To pray the night time through,

It was evening in Jerusalem,
And in the garden of Gethsemane,
The time and place in history was set,
To fulfill God's promise and prophecy,

Peter, James and John were there,
And he asked them all to pray,
He needed all the strength he could muster,
To face the events come next day,

He went ahead a stones throw,
And bowed his head in prayer,
Beseeching his father to remove the cup,
That he alone had to bear,

He came back to his men three times,
And found them all asleep,
But it didn't really matter now,
For it was time to scatter the sheep,

"The shepherd would be smitten,"
The prophecy did say,
"Then the sheep they would be scattered,
And they'd turn and run away,"

Now Judas told the soldiers
That he would give them a sign,
The one that he'd kiss in the garden,
Was the one they should seize and bind,

In the Beginning God

Then Judas walked up to him,
And greeted him with a kiss,
"Judas you betray me?" He said,
"In a manner such as this?"

A crowd armed with staves and clubs,
Approached him in the night,
He said, "You have found me let the others go,"
And he didn't put up a fight,

Judas never answered him,
He just turned and walked away,
And was paid thirty pieces of silver,
For betraying him that day,

Then Peter took his sword,
And he rose up to fight,
He smote the servant of the high priest,
And cut off his ear that night,

"Put away your sword," said Jesus,
Then he touched and healed the servant's ear,
He said, "He who lives by the sword dies by the same,"
And his men were filled with fear,

They scattered as they led him away,
To the palace of the high priest,
But Peter followed from far behind,
That night of the Passover feast,

A fire was kindling in the courtyard,
Peter sat and began to surmise,
He tried to look inconspicuous,
For fear that he'd be recognized,

"This man was also with him,"
"I know him not," was his reply,
They asked him again two more times,
And twice more he did deny,

While he yet spoke the cock crowed,
It was just as Jesus said,
Peter went out and wept bitterly,
Heart filled with sorrow and dread,

Then they blindfolded Jesus,
And struck him on his face,
They spit on him and told him to prophesy,
While the lawyers prepared their case,

The elders, scribes and chief priests,
Waited until it was day,
To the council is where they brought him,
As they whisked the Savior away,

And many false witnesses,
Came forward to testify,
"Art thou the Christ?" they asked him,
"If I said yes you wouldn't believe," was his reply,

"Art thou the son of God?" they asked,
"Thou hast said," he told the chief Pharisee,
"We need no further witnesses,
He is guilty of blasphemy!"

Then they quickly took him,
To another place,
They wanted to end his ministry,
So they brought him there in haste,

In the Beginning God

To the Roman Procurator,
Pontius Pilate was his name,
And there they all accused him,
"He perverts nation!" was their claim,

When Pilate saw him, he asked,
"Art thou the king of the Jews?"
He gave an affirmation,
And Pilate was confused,

When Pilate heard he was from Galilee,
He refused to hear the case,
After all he was a Galilean,
So the trial belonged at Herod's place,

When he arrived, Herod's men mocked him,
And laughed, "Ha King of the Jews,"
They adorned him in a purple robe,
And at his cost they were amused,

While he was with Herod,
The leaders mounted their attack,
But he answered not a word,
So King Herod sent him back,

Pilate called them together, and said,
"I find no guilt in this man,"
Even though he found no guilt,
This wouldn't reverse God's plan,

"I will therefore chastise him,
And then I'll let him go,"
The Leaders didn't agree,
Their reply was a vehement "No!"

John A. Lingenfelter

So Pilate ordered him flogged,
And as the whip did crack,
The lead nails on the end of it,
Ripped and tore at Jesus' back,

Each lash was more intense,
As he winced with pain,
It was the price he had to pay,
To remove sin's crimson stain,

Then they made crown of thorns,
And pressed it on his head,
They commented, "Every king needs a crown,"
As the savior profusely bled,

Pilate's wife Procula called him aside,
And she said, "I had a dream,
Have nothing to do with this just man,
Take no part in their scheme,"

Pilate asked him once again,
"Art thou the king of the Jews?"
"Though sayest," was his only answer,
Pilate marveled and was confused,

Then Pilate said, "Don't you hear,
What the witnesses say of thee?"
"Well say something to defend yourself!
Why don't you answer me?"

"Don't you know I have the power to release you!
Or to have you crucified!"
"The power you're given is from above,"
Jesus humbly replied,

In the Beginning God

"Therefore the one that delivers me,
Has the greater sin,"
So Pilate sought all the more to free him,
As he anguished deep within,

Now at the feast the Procurator,
Would grant an amnesty,
He'd release to them one prisoner,
So he thought he might set him free,

Pilate asked the crowd,
"Which man should I set free?"
"Choose your king Jesus or the convict Barabbas,"
And then he waited just to see,

And the people shouted, "Barabbas!"
He asked, "What about your King?"
"Away with him to be crucified!"
The shouts from the crowd did ring,

Many once shouted, "Hosanna!"
In a loud and supportive voice,
But today they chose a thief and murderer,
As their number one choice,

Then Pilate asked the crowd,
"Why, what evil has he done?"
But they shouted all the louder,
To crucify God's son,

Then when Pilate saw,
He couldn't convince the crowd,
For a riot was ensuing,
And their demands were very loud,

John A. Lingenfelter

Then Pilate washed his hands,
And proclaimed, to the multitude,
"I'm innocent of this just man's blood,"
The death sentence then ensued,

Then the crowd led Jesus away,
They gave him a cross to bear,
He was on his way to Calvary,
And the multitudes followed him there,

As he made his way,
Through the hostile street,
Some women of Jerusalem,
Fell and wept there at his feet,

Then he looked down at them,
As they stopped him on his way,
And said, "Do not weep for me, but for you
And your children on this day,"

Then a Roman soldier struck him,
So he continued up the road,
He carried the sins of the world,
And it was a heavy load,

His body was writhing in pain,
From the lashing he took that day,
And the cross was getting heavier
Each step along the way,

When they thought he couldn't make it,
They weren't at a loss,
They seized Simon of Cyrene,
And made him help him carry his cross,

In the Beginning God

Simon got right next to him,
And helped him bear the load,
And they aided one another,
On their way up Calvary's road,

Jesus nodded in appreciation,
As Simon helped him on the way,
"Come on it's just a little further,"
Simon said to him that day,

When they arrived at the top of Calvary's hill,
Somehow Simon wanted to stay,
He didn't understand what had happened,
Then the soldiers pushed him away,

Two thieves were also led there,
To be crucified,
One of the two repented,
And with his own punishment he complied,

Then the repentant thief asked him,
"Lord please, remember me?"
And Jesus said, "Truly this day,
In heaven you will be,"

Then they drove the nails,
Through his feet and wrist,
And Jesus felt the pain of sin,
And in anguish he did twist,

Then they hoisted the cross up,
When the last nail was pound,
And the people watched intently,
As they slammed it into the ground,

When it hit he moaned in anguish,
And then he hung there for two hours,
The people demanded, "Save yourself!"
And questioned all his powers,

Then he said, "Father forgive them,
For they know not what they do,"
And they continued then to rail him,
For his suffering was not yet through,

"My God, My God," he cried out,
"Why hast thou forsaken me?"
For even his Father had to turned his back,
To fulfill the prophesy,

There he hung cursed,
And what loneliness he felt,
He was the living embodiment of all man's sins,
This was the final lash from sin's belt,

"Father into your hands I give my spirit,"
Cried out, the Lord of hosts,
Thus the reign of death was over,
Once Jesus gave up the ghost,

Now according to the Mosaic Law,
Only the high priest could go,
In the temple's inner sanctuary to be with God,
But now this wasn't so,

The curtain that once divided it,
Was torn right in two,
Thus salvation's door was now open,
To **all** men like me and you,

In the Beginning God

So Jesus fulfilled the prophesy,
That was promised in Eden that day,
When he crushed the head of the serpent,
And washed our sins away,

Chapter 19
The Resurrection and Ascension
From the Gospels of Matthew, Chapters 27, 28
Mark, Chapters 15, 16 Luke, Chapters 23, 24 and
John, Chapters 18, 19, 20, 21

Joseph of Arimathaea,
Went to Pilate that same day,
He begged for the body of Jesus,
And was permitted to take him away,

Nicodemus also came,
To help lay him to rest,
They were two honorable Pharisees,
Just trying to do their best,

Joseph wrapped him in linen,
When he took him from the cross,
Nicodemus brought the anointing aloes,
And they stood and mourned their loss,

They laid him in an unused tomb,
That was hewn from rock,
Rolled a stone in front of it,
And both stood there in shock,

Then three days later,
Before the break of day,
Mary Magdalene and some other women came,
And saw the stone was rolled away,

In the Beginning God

So she ran and told Peter,
What she had surmised,
That they had taken the Lord away,
She would later be surprised,

Then Peter and another disciple,
Ran to the tomb to see,
They too believed he was taken,
For they knew not the prophesy,

That Messiah would rise again,
On the third day,
To get the victory over death,
And finally wash all sin away,

When Peter arrived he stooped down,
And beheld the linen clothes,
They laid there by themselves,
And Peter was at a loss,

Later Mary wept outside his tomb
And from behind she heard a voice,
It was Jesus he'd raised from the dead,
And in her heart she did rejoice,

Mary quickly told his men,
Who were hiding for fear of the Jews,
Thomas wasn't there that night,
So later he was told the news,

But Thomas didn't believe them,
Then when eight days had passed by,
He reappeared and Thomas said he believed,
"Only because you see," was Jesus' reply,

"Blessed are those who believe and haven't seen,"
He taught them all that day,
And although Thomas had doubted him,
Jesus loved him anyway,

He told them to love one another,
To preach the Gospel to all men,
And that he would always be with them,
Then he ascended to his Father again,

If the Pharisees had displayed his body,
After that third day,
Our faith, it would mean nothing,
And the stain of sin would stay,

But in Bethlehem city of David,
A babe had been born to you,
And so with Caesar's tax edicts,
The prophecies came true,

Who'd ever think that little boy,
Born in Bethlehem on that day,
Came to shed his blood and give his life,
Just to wash our sins away,

Oh he healed the sick, raised the dead,
And made many blind people see,
But he got the victory over sin and death,
When he died and rose for you and me,

Chapter 20
The Conclusion

For three years of his ministry,
People followed as he rose to fame,
He was the carpenter from Galilee,
And Jesus was his name,

Jesus the carpenter,
The best in all the trade,
The most unique of all his works,
The example of love that he made,

People shared as he fed five thousand,
Some saw that he was divine,
His first miracle was at a wedding feast,
Where he changed water into wine,

He healed the sick, raised the dead,
And made many blind people see,
He taught us love, gave the world hope,
And fulfilled the prophesies,

He showed us that history moves with purpose,
It's not a medley of random events,
Because all things that ever occur,
They play part in God's covenants,

Well now you've heard his story,
Hopefully, it doesn't seem so odd,
That the first four words of the Good Book,
Start with, "In the beginning God,"

John A. Lingenfelter

He's the Alpha and the Omega,
The beginning and the end,
His word it stands forever,
And it's not just part of some trend,

So when life calls for decision,
Before you make a choice,
Pray and search the scriptures,
And listen for God's voice,

For we know He keeps his promises,
To all those who would pray,
To men like Noah, Abraham and Moses,
That walked in faith each day,

For every man since Eden,
Has always had a choice,
To doubt God or walk in faith,
To curse life, or rejoice,

So pray a prayer of salvation,
And ask him into your heart,
Though the road sometimes may be rocky,
From your side he'll never part,

If you accept him as your Savior,
And believe that he died for you,
He'll embrace you at Salvation's gate,
And bid you to pass right through,

Chapter 21
The Prayer of Salvation

Lord Jesus, I repent of my sins.
I ask you to come into my heart.
I make you my Lord and Savior.

Amen.

If you would you like to order
In the Beginning God
Please complete and mail the order form below. Make check or money order payable to E-BookTime, LLC.

In the Beginning God ISBN 1-59824-287-3

Copies _____   Price Each $8.95   Total _____
Alabama residents add 4% sales tax: _____
Shipping and handling: $5.95
                    Net Total _____

___ Check or money order
___ Charge credit/debit card __ Visa __ Mastercard
Name on Card   _____
Billing Address   _____
                   _____
         City   _____
         State ___ ZIP _____
Card Number _____
Valid Through _____ / _____

Shipping Address if Different Than Billing Address
Name   _____
Address   _____
           _____
    City   _____
    State ___ ZIP _____

Note: We cannot ship to P.O. boxes.
Delivery contact phone number _____

Send To   E-BookTime, LLC
              6598 Pumpkin Road
              Montgomery, AL 36108

(Price and availability subject to change.)

Printed in the United States
57726LVS00008B/460-549